"THE PROPHET JEREMIAH"
IS A POWERFUL STUDY OF
A MAN IN DEEP THOUGHT.
IT IS A PAINTING OF A THINKER
AND A MAN OF ACTION.
MICHELANGELO MAKES
US AWARE OF JEREMIAH'S
PHYSICAL STRENGTH AND
READINESS THROUGH THE
POWERFUL LINES OF THE PROPHET'S

DETAIL: PROPHET JEREMIAH   SISTINE CHAPEL, VATICAN

SHOULDERS, ARMS, HANDS,
AND HEAVY BOOTED LEGS.

THE HANDS ARE THOSE OF
A WORKER, A DOER.

THE HEAD AND FACE ARE
THOSE OF A PHILOSOPHER
AND PROPHET.

IT IS BELIEVED THAT
MICHELANGELO
USED HIMSELF AS A
MODEL
FOR
JEREMIAH.

THE ALCHEMIST   BRITISH MUSEUM, LONDON

LORENZO DE'MEDICI   MEDICI CHAPEL, FLORENCE

DEDICATED TO PETER KRASNOW, ARTIST, AND TO ROSE,
HIS WIFE AND BIOGRAPHER

LIBRARY OF CONGRESS CATALOGING-IN-PUBLICATION DATA
RABOFF, ERNEST LLOYD.
    MICHELANGELO BUONARROTI.
    (ART FOR CHILDREN)
REPRINT. ORIGINALLY PUBLISHED: GARDEN CITY, N.Y.: DOUBLEDAY, 1971. SUMMARY: A BRIEF BIOGRAPHY OF MICHELANGELO BUONARROTI ACCOMPANIES
FOURTEEN COLOR REPRODUCTIONS AND CRITICAL INTERPRETATIONS OF HIS WORKS. 1. MICHELANGELO BUONARROTI, 1475-1564 - JUVENILE LITERATURE.
2. PAINTERS - ITALY - BIOGRAPHY - JUVENILE LITERATURE. 3. PAINTING, ITALIAN - JUVENILE LITERATURE. 4. PAINTING, RENAISSANCE - ITALY -
JUVENILE LITERATURE. [1. MICHELANGELO BUONARROTI, 1475-1564. 2. ARTISTS. 3. PAINTING, ITALIAN. 4. PAINTING, RENAISSANCE -
ITALY] I. TITLE. II. SERIES. ND683.B9R3 1988   759.5   [92]   87-45313   ISBN 0-397-32223-2

MICHELANGELO
BUONARROTI

By Ernest Raboff

ART
FOR
CHILDREN

J. B. LIPPINCOTT · NEW YORK

MICHELANGELO WAS BORN NEARLY
500 YEARS AGO IN CAPRESE, ITALY, ON MARCH 6, 1475.
HIS FATHER, LUDOVICI DI LEONARDO DI BUONARROTI, WAS
ACTING MAGISTRATE OF THE TOWN. AFTER MICHELANGELO'S
BIRTH THE FAMILY RETURNED HOME TO FLORENCE.

AT THE AGE OF 13 THE YOUTH WAS APPRENTICED TO THE
WELL KNOWN ARTIST GHIRLANDAIO AND FROM HIM
LEARNED THE ART OF MURAL PAINTING. AFTER ONE
YEAR'S APPRENTICESHIP MICHELANGELO WAS INVITED BY
LORENZO DE' MEDICI (CALLED "THE MAGNIFICENT"), RULER
OF FLORENCE, TO STUDY AND WORK IN THE SCHOOL OF
SCULPTURE HE HAD FOUNDED IN THE PALACE GARDENS.

HIS PATRON, LORENZO, DIED WHEN MICHELANGELO WAS 17.
FROM THAT DAY ON HE WORKED INDEPENDENTLY FOR MANY
OF THE RULERS AND RELIGIOUS LEADERS OF FLORENCE,
BOLOGNA, AND ROME. AT THE AGE OF 24 HIS SCULPTURE CALLED
THE "PIETA," OF THE MADONNA AND
JESUS, MADE HIM FAMOUS. LATER
HE WAS TO PAINT HIS CONCEPT OF
THE CREATION OF THE WORLD ON
THE CEILING OF ROME'S SISTINE
CHAPEL.

FROM HIS NOBLE MIND AND CREATIVE
HANDS CAME MASTERPIECE AFTER
MASTERPIECE. MICHELANGELO
WORKED AS PAINTER, SCULPTOR,
ARCHITECT, AND POET UNTIL
THE AGE OF ALMOST 90
WHEN HE DIED IN ROME ON
FEBRUARY 18, 1564.

PORTRAIT OF THE ARTIST BY ERNEST RABOFF

MICHELANGELO

IS QUOTED BY HIS FRIEND, GIANNOTTI, AS SAYING, "I HAVE ALWAYS TAKEN DELIGHT IN CONVERSING WITH LEARNED PERSONS..."

"WHENEVER I SEE SOMEONE WHO IS GOOD FOR SOMETHING, WHO SHOWS SOME POWER OF THE MIND, WHO CAN DO OR SAY SOMETHING BETTER THAN THE OTHERS, I AM COMPELLED TO FALL IN LOVE WITH HIM..."

ANOTHER WRITER, BERTONI, SAID, "MICHELANGELO DID NOT HAVE A LITERARY MAN'S STYLE, NOR ANY WORDS THAT WERE NOT HIS OWN, ALL HIS OWN, THAT IS, ROOTED IN HIS SOUL..."

MICHELANGELO'S LETTERS ARE FILLED WITH NOBLE THOUGHTS AND GOOD ADVICE. "MEN ARE WORTH MORE THAN MONEY." "GOING SLOWLY YOU MAKE FEWER MISTAKES..."

PIER SODERINI KNEW HIM AS: "A FINE YOUTH AND IN HIS CRAFT UNIQUE IN ITALY, PERHAPS IN THE WHOLE UNIVERSE.

HE IS OF SUCH NATURE THAT WITH FAIR WORDS AND KINDNESS ...HE WILL DO ANYTHING..."

PIETA   DUOMO, FLORENCE

"THE HOLY FAMILY" (CALLED THE DONI TONDO) WAS PAINTED TO HONOR THE MARRIAGE OF AGNOLO DONI. UNTIL THIS WORK MICHELANGELO WAS KNOWN PRIMARILY FOR HIS SCULPTURE. ON THE SIDE OF A SKETCH FOR THIS PAINTING, THE 29 YEAR OLD ARTIST WROTE, "WHO WOULD EVER SAY THAT THIS WORK WAS BY MY HAND?"

IN THIS OIL PAINTING, THE HOLY FAMILY SEEMS CARVED OUT OF STONE. THE BACKGROUND IS PAINTED AS A SEPARATE MURAL MAKING A HUMAN SETTING FOR THE HOLY MOTHER, FATHER AND CHILD.

THE GLOBAL

SHAPE

OF THE PAINTING
ENCOMPASSES
BOTH

HEAVEN

AND

EARTH.

MADONNA, CHILD AND SAINT JOHN,
BRITISH MUSEUM, LONDON

DONI TONDO   UFFIZI GALLERY, FLORENCE

"MOSES", ONE OF MICHELANGELO'S MOST IMPRESSIVE WORKS, TOOK FOUR YEARS TO CARVE FROM A HUGE BLOCK OF MARBLE.

THIS WORK REQUIRED YEARS OF STUDY, INCLUDING THE COPYING OF ANCIENT GREEK AND ROMAN SCULPTURE. YET THE ARTIST GAVE HIS OWN PERSONALITY AND PHILOSOPHY TO THE CARVING.

MOSES, LAW-GIVER AND RECEIVER OF THE TEN COMMANDMENTS (SHOWN UNDER HIS ARM), WAS THE LEADER OF HIS PEOPLE.

HIS HORNS ARE LIKE ANTENNAS TAKING IN WISDOM FROM THE HEAVENS.

CARVED OWL

HIS FACE SEEMS LIKE A LAND-SCAPE. THE EYES ARE LIGHTS — THE SUN AND THE MOON WATCH-FUL DAY AND NIGHT. HIS BROW AND NOSE ARE PROTECTIVE MOUNTAIN RANGES. HIS MOUTH IS A WELL, FILLED WITH WISE WORDS, AND HIS BEARD, A GARDEN OF VINES. THE DEEP LINES ARE FURROWS PLOWED BY CONCERN FOR HIS PEOPLE. MOSES' BODY, IN THE PRIME OF LIFE, IS A FORTRESS OF STRENGTH.

PORTRAIT OF ANDREA QUARATESI, BRITISH MUSEUM

MOSES   CHURCH OF SAN PIETRO IN VINCOLI, ROME

"THE ERYTHRAEAN SIBYL" WAS ONE OF THE TWELVE FEMALE PROPHETS CALLED SIBYLS, WHO IN THE AGES BEFORE CHRISTIANITY, FORETOLD THE FUTURE. MICHELANGELO PAINTED FIVE SUCH SIBYLS ALONG THE CEILING OF THE SISTINE CHAPEL IN THE VATICAN.

SHE IS A GODDESS-LIKE FIGURE OF CALMNESS AND STRENGTH. THE ARTIST PAINTED HER AS HAVING BOTH PURPOSE AND STATURE. IT WAS SHE WHO PREDICTED THE LAST JUDGMENT OF MANKIND, THE SUBJECT OF MICHELANGELO'S FAMOUS MURAL ON THE ALTAR WALL OF THE VATICAN CHAPEL.

HER FACE IS ROUND. HER EYE GAZES AT HER BOOK OF PROPHECIES. HER MOUTH IS TENDER. HER BRAIDED HAIR AND THE RIM OF HER COLORFUL HEAD-DRESS FOLLOW THE SAME SOFT LINES AS THE GARMENTS THAT DRAPE SOFTLY AROUND HER BODY IN SWIRLS OF WHITE, BLUE GOLD AND PURPLE.

MADONNA AND CHILD   BRITISH MUSEUM, LONDON

ERYTHRAEAN SIBYL   SISTINE CHAPEL, ROME

"ST. PROCULUS", THE STATUE OF A DETERMINED YOUNG CHRISTIAN, WAS CREATED FOR THE TOMB OF SAINT DOMINICK WHEN MICHELANGELO, AN EQUALLY DETERMINED YOUTH, WAS ONLY 19 YEARS OLD. HERE WE SEE A FACE THAT IS RESOLUTE AND A BODY POISED TO MEET LIFE'S CHALLENGES.

FIFTY YEARS AFTER FINISHING THIS SCULPTURE, MICHELANGELO WROTE: "...PAINTING AND SCULPTURE ARE ONE AND THE SAME THING...EVERY PAINTER SHOULD NOT FAIL TO DO SCULPTURE AS WELL AS PAINTING; AND LIKEWISE, THE SCULPTOR. I MEAN BY SCULPTURE THAT WHICH IS DONE BY TAKING AWAY; THAT WHICH IS DONE BY ADDING IS LIKE PAINTING."

WE CAN ALMOST SEE THIS STURDY MUSCULAR BODY ALIVE AND MOVING BENEATH ITS MARBLE CLOTHING.

ST. PROCULUS   SAN DOMENICO, BOLOGNA

DETAIL, HEADS FOR THE JUDGEMENT   BRITISH MUSEUM, LONDON

"THE DELPHIC SIBYL"
IN ANCIENT GREEK
MYTHOLOGY WAS THE
MOST FAMOUS TELLER
OF FORTUNES. SHE
WAS THE VOICE OF
APOLLO, THE GREEK
GOD OF MUSIC, POETRY,
PROPHECY AND
MEDICINE.

MICHELANGELO IN
THIS DETAIL FROM HIS
PAINTING IN THE SISTINE
CHAPEL, SHOWS US THIS HANDSOME WOMAN HOLDING A
PROPHETIC SCROLL IN HER RAISED LEFT HAND WHILE HER
EYES GAZE PAST US INTO THE FUTURE.

THE FOUR COLORS USED BY MICHELANGELO IN
HER GARMENTS COULD REPRESENT THE
EARTH, FIRE, WATER AND AIR —
THE KNOWN ELEMENTS OF LIFE ON THIS PLANET.

PERHAPS THE CHILDREN BEHIND HER ARE READING
HER BOOK TO DISCOVER THEIR OWN PROPHETIC
FUTURES.

THE DELPHIC SIBYL   SISTINE CHAPEL, ROME

"VIRGIN OF THE STAIRS", A MARBLE RELIEF, IS
BELIEVED TO HAVE BEEN CREATED BY MICHELANGELO
WHEN HE WAS 16 YEARS OLD. HE ONCE SAID, "AS A
BABY I WAS NURSED BY A STONE-CUTTER'S WIFE AND I
TOOK IN WITH MY NURSE'S MILK THE CHISELS AND THE
HAMMERS I USE IN MY SCULPTURE."

IN THIS EARLY MASTERPIECE OF A YOUNG BOY NURSING,
HE HAS GIVEN US THE MAN THE CHILD WILL BECOME
IN THE MUSCULAR FORMS OF THE NECK, SHOULDERS,
BACK AND ARM.

THE CALM FACE OF THE NURSING MOTHER PERHAPS
GAZES INTO THE FUTURE OF HER CHILD.

DETAIL, VIRGIN OF THE STAIRS

VIRGIN OF THE STAIRS   CASA BUONARROTI, FLORENCE

"THE PROPHET JOEL"

IS ONE OF SEVEN ANCIENT HEBREW **SEERS** THAT MICHELANGELO PAINTED ON THE CEILING OF THE SISTINE CHAPEL. LIKE THE FIVE **SIBYLS**, THEY WERE CHARACTERS IN THE HISTORY OF WESTERN RELIGION. JOEL WAS A WRITER WHO WROTE THAT GOD WAS A

STUDIES FOR THE DOME AND LANTERN OF ST. PETER'S
TEYLER MUSEUM, HAARLEM

KIND AND COMPASSIONATE BEING. THE ARTIST HAS SHOWN HIM AS A SERIOUS BUT GENTLE MAN. IT IS BELIEVED THAT A COLLEAGUE, DONATO BRAMANTE, THE ARCHITECT OF ST. PETER'S CATHEDRAL, WAS HIS MODEL FOR THIS PROPHET.

JOEL IS SHOWN READING FROM A SCROLL WHICH FORMS A LINE FROM ONE HAND TO THE OTHER ACROSS THE PAINTING. MICHELANGELO OFTEN DESIGNED HIS WORKS IN THE LINES OF A **CROSS** WITHIN A **PYRAMID**.

STUDIES OF A CAPITAL   CASA BUONARROTI, FLORENCE

PROPHET JOEL   SISTINE CHAPEL, ROME

"GUILIANO DE' MEDICI" WAS A MEMBER OF THE FAMOUS FAMILY THAT RULED FLORENCE, ITALY, FOR MANY YEARS. THIS MARBLE STATUE WAS CREATED FOR THE MEDICI CHAPEL.

GUILIANO HAS BEEN CARVED WEARING THE TUNIC OF A ROMAN GENERAL. THE SCEPTER OF COMMAND LIES GENTLY IN HIS SENSITIVE HANDS. THE THUMB AND FIRST FINGER OF HIS LEFT HAND HOLD A COIN. IT IS BELIEVED MICHELANGELO PUT IT THERE TO SHOW THE MEDICI'S RESPECT FOR AND GENEROSITY TOWARD ALL MEN OF THOUGHT, SCIENCE, LETTERS AND ART.

THE ARTIST'S GENIUS FOR USING HIS HAMMERS, CHISELS AND POLISHING STONES IS SHOWN IN THE DETAILS AND MOVEMENT OF THE STATUE'S GARMENT AND IN THE MUSCULAR FORMS OF THE BODY.

GUILIANO, WHO WAS ALSO A BROTHER OF POPE LEO X, IS PORTRAYED BY THIS MASTER SCULPTOR AS A MAN WHOSE INTELLIGENT FACE HAS BOTH SENSITIVITY AND STRENGTH.

HEAD OF A BEARDED MAN   BRITISH MUSEUM

GUILIANO DE' MEDICI   CHURCH OF SAN LORENZO, FLORENCE

"THE PROPHET JOSIAH" AND HIS FAMILY FORM A TRIANGLE
FILLING A VAULT ON THE CEILING OF THE SISTINE CHAPEL.

THE **FATHER** IS THE BASE OF THE FAMILY PYRAMID.
THE MOTHER AND CHILD FORM THE TWO SIDES.

MICHELANGELO, LIKE ALL GREAT PAINTERS, USES LINES,
COLORS, FORMS AND SPACES AS A WRITER USES WORDS AND
PHRASES TO GIVE STRUCTURAL BEAUTY, DESIGN AND
MEANING TO HIS **THOUGHTS.**

THE MOTHER'S STRENGTH IS HIDDEN BENEATH THE FOLDS
OF HER WHITE VEIL AND HER PURPLE ROBE. SHE SITS
UPON HER GRASS GREEN SHAWL, ITS END CURLED IN
HER LAP, CLOSE TO THE **BROWN EARTH**. THE GOLD,
BLUE AND WHITE CLOTHING OF JOSIAH MIGHT REPRESENT
THE CHARACTER OF HIS SOUL, THE
BEAUTY OF HIS MIND AND THE
PEACEFUL NATURE OF HIS PERSONALITY.

THE MOTHER'S ARMS CLASP THE
CHILD IN A SOFT EMBRACE. THE
CHILD'S LEFT ARM CURLS IN A SOFT

ARC

FINDING SECURITY
BETWEEN
HIS RESTING PARENTS.

DETAIL FROM STUDIES OF CHERUBS
BRITISH MUSEUM, LONDON

PROPHET JOSIAH   SISTINE CHAPEL, ROME

RHYMES (1511)

"THE PROPHET ISAIAH"
WAS A HEBREW SEER
ABLE TO LOOK INTO THE
FUTURE.

MICHELANGELO BUONARROTI
WAS A STUDENT OF THE BIBLE.
HE USED ITS STORIES AND
ITS PEOPLE FOR HIS
PAINTING AND SCULPTURE.

IN THE BOOK WHICH ISAIAH
HOLDS OPEN WITH HIS RIGHT HAND IT IS WRITTEN:
"...OUT OF THEIR GLOOM AND DARKNESS THE EYES
OF THE BLIND SHALL SEE." LATER IN THE SAME VERSE
HE SAYS: "IN QUIETNESS AND
TRUST THERE SHALL BE STRENGTH".
FOR MICHELANGELO THERE
WAS DEEP MEANING IN THE
PROPHET'S WORDS.

BOOKS, WHICH ARE SEEN IN
MANY OF MICHELANGELO'S
WORKS, BROUGHT HIM FAME
AS A SCHOLAR AND POET.

HERE, ISAIAH TURNS FROM HIS
BOOK TO LISTEN TO A CHILD.

RHYMES (AFTER 1546)

PROPHET ISAIAH   SISTINE CHAPEL, ROME

"THE BRUGES MADONNA" IS A BEAUTIFUL EXAMPLE OF THE 26 YEAR OLD MICHELANGELO'S GENIUS. HIS ABILITY TO CREATE ALMOST MAKES OUR EYES BELIEVE THAT THIS MARBLE STATUE LIVES. IF WE SHOULD TOUCH THE MOTHER'S DRESS, IT SEEMS AS THOUGH IT WOULD MOVE BENEATH OUR FINGERS.

THE MADONNA'S FACE IS CALM AND THOUGHTFUL. IT GLOWS LIKE A MOON ABOVE THE PYRAMID OF HER BODY. HER GRACEFUL ARMS FORM THE SIDES OF THE PYRAMID. THE LINE THAT CURVES FROM HER RIGHT HAND TO THE CHILD'S FOREARM, AND THEN CONTINUES TO THE MOTHER'S LEFT HAND FORMS THE BASE OF THIS TRIANGULAR DESIGN.

THE BOY'S HEAD AND TORSO DECORATE ONE SIDE OF THIS PYRAMID; THE MOTHER'S DRESS THE OTHER.

DETAILS FROM "THE BRUGES MADONNA"

BRUGES MADONNA   CATHEDRAL OF NOTRE DAME, PARIS

DETAIL, THE PROPHET ZACHARIUS

"THE PROPHET ZACHARIAS" WAS THE FIRST PROPHET THAT MICHELANGELO PAINTED ON THE WALL OF THE SISTINE CHAPEL.

POPE JULIUS II, WHO BROUGHT MICHELANGELO TO ROME, IS SAID TO HAVE BEEN THE MODEL FOR THIS POWERFUL PORTRAIT.

THE CLOSE-CROPPED HAIR, MAJESTIC WHITE BEARD, AND THE LINED FACE OF THE PROPHET ARE THOSE OF A MAN WISE WITH AGE.

HIS FIRM HANDS LEAF THROUGH HIS BOOK AS THOUGH SEARCHING FOR AN IMPORTANT LESSON TO READ TO THE YOUNG STUDENTS WHO PEER OVER HIS SHOULDER.

THE PROPHET'S FLOWING GARMENTS FORM A SOLID BASE AROUND HIS SEATED FIGURE. HIS HEAD IS CENTERED ABOVE THE GOLDEN ARC MADE BY HIS RIGHT ARM.

DETAIL OF SIBYL AND OTHER STUDIES
DETROIT INSTITUTE OF ART

PROPHET ZACHARIAS   SISTINE CHAPEL, ROME